This Journal Belongs To:

_____

inspire

She
believed
SHE COULD
so she
did

_____

_____

_____

_____

_____

_____

_____

_____

_____

_____

_____

_____

_____

Notes

_____

_____

_____

_____

_____

_____

_____

_____

_____

Notes	*Notes*

Notes

Live FOR yourself

Notes

_____

_____

_____

_____

_____

_____

_____

_____

_____

_____

| Notes | Notes |

live
MORE
worry
LeSS

Notes

every moment matters

Notes

It's just a bad day, Not a bad life

Good things take time

_____

_____

_____

_____

_____

_____

_____

_____

_____

_____

_____

Notes

_____

_____

_____

_____

_____

_____

_____

_____

_____

Notes	*Notes*

Live
WHAT YOU
Love

Notes

Notes

Passion
Over
Perfection

_____

_____

_____

_____

_____

_____

_____

_____

_____

_____

_____

Notes

the best
is yet
to come

Notes

Notes

Notes

Notes

Notes

the universe is immaterial

_____

_____

_____

_____

_____

_____

_____

_____

_____

_____

_____

_____

_____

Notes

Notes

Notes

Notes

Do what
makes
you
Happy

Notes

You
become
what
You
☙ believe ☙

_____

_____

_____

_____

_____

_____

_____

_____

_____

_____

_____

_____

Notes	*Notes*

Each failure brings you one step closer to success

_____

_____

_____

_____

_____

_____

_____

_____

_____

_____

_____

Notes

IT Always SEEMS Impossible UNTIL IT'S DONE

_____

_____

_____

_____

_____

_____

_____

_____

_____

_____

_____

Notes	Notes

Notes

Notes

Live
FOR
yourself

_____

_____

_____

_____

_____

_____

_____

_____

_____

_____

_____

_____

_____

_____

_____

_____

_____

_____

Notes

_____

_____

_____

_____

_____

_____

_____

_____

_____

Notes	*Notes*

live
MORE
worry
LESS

Notes

every moment matters

_____

_____

_____

_____

_____

_____

_____

_____

_____

_____

_____

_____

_____

_____

_____

Notes